S0-BFI-168

First Board of General Superintendents
(l. to r.): E. P. Ellyson, Phineas F. Bresee,
and Hiram F. Reynolds.

Holiness unto the Lord

General Superintendents of the Church of the Nazarene

Paul W. Thornhill

Nazarene Publishing House
Kansas City, Missouri

Copyright 1997
by Nazarene Publishing House

ISBN 083-411-6707

Printed in the
United States of America

Cover design: Mike Walsh

Unless otherwise indicated, all Scripture quotations are from the *Holy Bible, New International Version®* (NIV®). Copyright © 1973, 1978, 1984 by International Bible Society. Used by permission of Zondervan Publishing House. All rights reserved.

Permission to quote from the following additional version is acknowledged with appreciation:
New American Standard Bible (NASB), © 1960, 1962, 1963, 1968, 1971, 1972, 1973, 1975, 1977 by The Lockman Foundation.

Scripture quotations marked KJV are from the King James Version.

Library of Congress Cataloging-in-Publication Data

Holiness unto the Lord: General Superintendents of the Church of the
    Nazarene / [compiled by] Paul W. Thornhill.
        p.   cm.
    ISBN 0-8341-1670-7 (pbk.)
    1. Church of the Nazarene. General Superintendents—History.
    2. Holiness—History of doctrines—19th century. 3. Holiness—History of doctrines—20th century. 4. Church of the Nazarene—Doctrines—History. 5. Holiness churches—Doctrines—History. I.
    Thornhill, Paul W.
    BX8699.N33G464   1997
    287.9'9'0922—dc21
        [B]   97-12150
                                                                        CIP

10   9   8   7   6   5   4   3   2   1

Quotes on Holiness
from the General Superintendents

Phineas F. Bresee: A sanctified life is a delight to Jesus, a joy to the soul, a benediction to the home, a power in the church, a terror to sin, and a continual disappointment to the devil (*Nazarene*, February 1, 1900).

Hiram F. Reynolds: This is the gospel that Paul preached, that Jesus has power to save men and women from their sin and sanctify them wholly—take sin out of them (sermon preached at Providence, Rhode Island, March 29, 1931).

E. P. Ellyson: The life of holiness is a life wholly under the mastery of the Spirit, a life of obedience to His leading (*Bible Holiness*, 1938).

E. F. Walker: Every true saint grows upward in heavenly-mindedness; downward in humility; inward in spirituality; and outward in a holy life and active usefulness (*Sanctify Them*, 1899).

W. C. Wilson: Let us look up into the face of God, recognizing Him as our Father, Jesus as our Elder Brother, the Holy Ghost as an indwelling Guide and Comforter ("Our Equipments," prepared and read by W. C. Wilson for the Epworth League Convention, Paducah, Kentucky, 1896).

J. W. Goodwin: Our sanctification must embrace a purification of our very nature from the defilement of sin, a cleansing from depravity of indwelling sin that we may fulfill the holy purpose for which we are called (*Living Signs and Wonders*, 1923).

R. T. Williams: When God sanctifies a soul, He cleanses the heart from all sin, destroys the old man, kills out sinful self and worldly ambitions, and fills the soul with love to God and man, against which there is no law (*Sanctification: The Experience and the Ethics*, 1928).

J. B. Chapman: Perhaps it is well that we should remember the exhortation of Paul to "walk in the Spirit." It is not enough that we have received Him and that He has sanctified us. We must continually recognize His presence, court His favor, and seek earnestly always to please Him (*Holy Spirit*, n.d.).

J. G. Morrison: The second work of grace is able to place us where we are saved to the uttermost, whether it be the uttermost of sin's depravity and inbred taint, or whether it be the uttermost boundary of sin's extension (*The Nazarene Pulpit*, 1925).

H. V. Miller: The baptism with the Holy Ghost by Jesus in the life of the believer, who will have it so, is the actual saturating of that personality with the divine presence until the very warp and woof of life takes a divine cast and from then on identifies its relationship to deity (*When He Is Come*, 1941).

Orval J. Nease: It is a commentary on what God has made us that while God is infinite, absolute, and divine, and we are but human, limited, and finite, God has so capacitated us that it takes what the infinite God is to satisfy what we are (*Heroes of Temptation*, 1945).

Hardy C. Powers: We simply declare our faith that the atonement of Jesus Christ, brought within reach of the consecrated, believing soul, is an adequate remedy for all sin (*Go Ye Next Door*, 1955).

G. B. Williamson: Man can know sanctifying grace only in a personal relationship to Christ made possible through the work of the Holy Spirit in man (*Sermons for Holiness Evangelism*, 1974).

Samuel Young: The genius of the Early Christian Church was its informal missions. Its zeal could not be contained. The gospel was spread by amateurs. They involved their time. This seems to be the best way even in our day. We dare not say even secretly— and never with contempt or conceit—"Who? Me?" (*Giving and Living*, 1974).

D. I. Vanderpool: Our only hope is a stirred spirit! Not mechanics, but dynamics; not better organization, better ritual, better buildings, finer choirs, or more money, but men and women— preachers and laymen—with Christ-stirred spirits (*Herald of Holiness*, July 16, 1951).

Hugh C. Benner: Our historical pattern is clear, and the same worldwide vision that moved the hearts of early Nazarenes characterizes the present-day Church of the Nazarene. We are under the divine commission to proceed aggressively to bear the glorious message to men everywhere that through Jesus Christ sinners can be converted and Christian believers can be sanctified wholly and "filled with the Holy Spirit" (*Herald of Holiness*, March 11, 1953).

V. H. Lewis: In sanctification there is no rebellion of the redeemed soul against the Holy Spirit. The intent of the Spirit-filled man is to obey God and live a life of service as God shall direct (*No Man Can Serve Two Masters*, 1964).

George Coulter: Holiness preaching confirmed by holiness living—the ultimate for God's man (*The Preacher's Magazine*, April 1977).

Edward G. Lawlor: We must be sure of our call and keep its surety clear—personally experiencing the fullness of the Spirit of holiness, basking in and constantly instructing ourselves in the nature of holiness (*The Preacher's Magazine*, October 1974).

Eugene L. Stowe: The nature of sin is so entrenched in human nature that only the deep cleansing provided by the blood of Jesus Christ through the agency of the powerful Holy Spirit can destroy it. The sanctifying, cleansing baptism with the Holy Spirit is still God's will for every believer (*Sanctify Them . . . That the World May Know*, 1987).

Orville W. Jenkins: A holy life is every preacher's badge of authority, and his shield of protection for living pure in a sinfully stained world (*The Preacher's Magazine*, September 1975).

Charles H. Strickland: Holiness in character is God's greatest achievement. Jesus has paid for our complete restoration, and the door is now open to "serve him without fear, in holiness and righteousness before him, all the days of our life" [Luke 1:74-75, KJV] (*Sanctify Them . . . That the World May Know*, 1987).

William M. Greathouse: Holiness is the work and gift of the triune God. The Father wills and plans our holiness; the Son reveals and provides holiness; the Spirit imparts holiness (*Herald of Holiness*, March 1996).

Jerald D. Johnson: It's true: "Holiness unto the Lord" has been, is now, and must forever be "our watchword and song" (*Herald of Holiness*, May 15, 1988).

John A. Knight: The Spirit gives the gift of being as well as doing: being together, the church not only has but is a support system. In the church joys are shared and burdens are borne. There is a sharing and caring life together in which the people of God dwell in the joyful unity of the Spirit (*Herald of Holiness*, August 15, 1988).

Raymond W. Hurn: Our service must be more than servanthood. It must be joyful servanthood, a servanthood that is motivated by love. Joyful service saves, and it fulfills (*Go . . . Preach*, 1992).

William J. Prince: An authentic faith in Christ Jesus produces some vital changes in the soul and lifestyle of the believer. One of the results of the Spirit-filled, sanctified life is love. Love for God and His Word leads the sanctified to righteousness and holiness (*Herald of Holiness*, August 1994).

Donald D. Owens: Christianity has always affirmed that human nature can be radically and permanently changed by the grace of God (*Go . . . Preach*, 1992).

James H. Diehl: We are sanctified by faith just as we are saved by faith. We don't earn our way in, merit our way in, struggle our way in, or work our way in. We believe our way in (*Herald of Holiness*, June 1996).

Paul G. Cunningham: We understand that whatever the church becomes in A.D. 2000 and beyond will in large part be determined by our willingness to passionately perpetuate the mission God has given us to proclaim Christian holiness (*Herald of Holiness*, July 1995).

General Superintendents of the Church of the Nazarene and Their Tenure of Service

Phineas F. Bresee, 1895-1915

Hiram F. Reynolds, 1907-32

E. P. Ellyson, 1908-11

E. F. Walker, 1911-18

W. C. Wilson, 1915

J. W. Goodwin, 1916-40

R. T. Williams, 1916-46

J. B. Chapman, 1928-47

J. G. Morrison, 1936-39

H. V. Miller, 1940-48

Orval J. Nease, 1940-44; 1948-50

Hardy C. Powers, 1944-68

G. B. Williamson, 1946-68

Samuel Young, 1948-72

D. I. Vanderpool, 1949-64

Hugh C. Benner, 1952-68

V. H. Lewis, 1960-85

George Coulter, 1964-80

Edward G. Lawlor, 1968-76

Eugene L. Stowe, 1968-93

Orville W. Jenkins, 1968-85

Charles H. Strickland, 1972-88

William M. Greathouse, 1976-89

Jerald D. Johnson, 1980-97

John A. Knight, 1985-

Raymond W. Hurn, 1985-93

William J. Prince, 1989-

Donald D. Owens, 1989-97

James H. Diehl, 1993-

Paul G. Cunningham, 1993-

Foreword

In the providence of God, Phineas F. Bresee and a group of 135 charter members walked "out under the stars" and became the first Church of the Nazarene in 1895. Those early Nazarenes doubtless had no idea of what would happen in the next 100 years. Many probably wondered if they could survive, but there is no doubt that they had a hope, a vision, and a dream to spread scriptural holiness to Los Angeles and the world.

From its incipiency the Church of the Nazarene was a people concerned about people. Our early church fathers sensed the voice of God speaking to them to "come out from among them, and be ye separate" (2 Cor. 6:17, KJV). There was an urgency that we should preach the new birth until people everywhere know that they must be born again and that we should lift high the banner of "holiness unto the Lord" until all people know that the individual can be cleansed from all sin.

The Church of the Nazarene has experienced phenomenal growth in its 100-year existence. We have added to those 135 charter members to the point at which our membership now stands at more than 1.2 million. Since the beginning of our denomination, 30 men have served in the capacity of general superintendent, which is the highest elective office of the church. These men who have graced this office have come from varied backgrounds in ministry, education, and service. However, all have had a heart for people, a passion for souls, and a message of holiness to preach. This book shares a glimpse into the hearts of the men who have led our great church.

The Church of the Nazarene is still a people concerned about people. The Board of General Superintendents still calls the church, both clergy and laity, to pursue the challenge "that the world may know." This is not the time for digging into our retreats; it is a time in the history of humanity to rise up as people of God to proclaim the good news of Jesus Christ as the Savior and Hope of the world. Something must happen in our hearts and minds so that we recognize that the most important thing we can do is to "go . . . into all the world, and preach the gospel" (Mark 16:15, KJV).

Founding General Superintendent Phineas F. Bresee saw before the Church of the Nazarene an open door a century ago and conceived the idea that she was in the sunrise of her history. Bresee often shouted to the congregation, "The sun never sets in the morning!" It is still morning in the Church of the Nazarene, and now the sun never sets on the Church of the Nazarene around the globe.

—William J. Prince
Chairman,
Board of General Superintendents

Introduction

In spite of outside influences, secular and even satanic, which endeavor to erode the foundations upon which the Church rests, we take heart in a declaration of the Lord, "I will build my church" (Matt. 16:18). It is His. He is building it. This assurance gives confidence and joy as we plan and pray for the future.

"The Church's one Foundation / Is Jesus Christ, her Lord" (Samuel J. Stone), and "the gates of hell shall not prevail against it" (Matt. 16:18, KJV).

Jerald D. Johnson

—Jerald D. Johnson
General Superintendent

The visible, organized Church is the most significant institution on the earth. It is initiated by God, loved by Christ, and established by the Holy Spirit. It is composed of men and women whose "hearts" have been "sprinkled from an evil conscience" (Heb. 10:22, KJV).

Because it is built on the Word of God, Jesus said, "The gates of hell shall not prevail against it" (Matt. 16:18, KJV). The Church retains its identity by faithfully proclaiming the gospel.

The Church of the Nazarene, a part of the total Body of Christ, does not claim to be the sole agency of the gospel—but she does have a glorious message of *full salvation*.

One does not have to be a Nazarene to be saved at the last day, but being a Nazarene who is saved is a prized heritage.

May the International Church of the Nazarene fulfill her destiny by continuing to be a "Great Commission movement" into the 21st century.

John A. Knight

—John A. Knight
General Superintendent

The Church of the Nazarene, with its sound biblical teachings, its commitment to world evangelism, and its investment in higher education, can and must have a moral impact on society. The world always pulls at the believer to travel the low road of indifference and lovelessness, but God calls us to the high way of holiness and righteousness.

The call of God to His people is still "You shall consecrate yourselves therefore and be holy, for I am the LORD your God. And you shall keep My statutes and practice them; I am the LORD who sanctifies you" (Lev. 20:7-8, NASB).

—William J. Prince
General Superintendent

A new millennium of history and opportunities awaits the Church of the Nazarene. The power that generates our global movement lies in our ability to march to the same drumbeat of the sanctifying Spirit, living in His constant embrace and empowerment. According to Acts 1:8, our all-conquering Christ has a global perspective in His redemptive designs.

The power and impetus of our movement, the powerful engine that has driven us for these 100 years, has been our attention to carrying out the Great Commission. The core of competencies in Holiness evangelism and mission has resulted in our effective witness in 116 world areas. We must perpetually create and excite a global outlook that engages the gifts of our people all around the world on a daily basis. And never on a "them and us" basis! A global vision compels us to clarify our global strategies and share a global culture with the same beliefs, attitudes, values, and expectations.

This requires a high level of trust. We must believe that the Holy Spirit does not limit His prevenience, His power, and His plans to North American Christianity.

—Donald D. Owens
General Superintendent

It has been 102 years since Los Angeles and 89 years since Pilot Point. What a glorious century for the Church of the Nazarene! From our very humble beginnings to churches now in 116 countries of the world; from a missionary vision proclaimed by our early leaders to over 1.2 million members worldwide; from a modest building or two to over 12,000 churches, 45 Bible colleges and seminaries, and 37 medical clinics and hospitals—the anointing of God has been upon the church!

But what about the future, and where will the younger generation take us? After attending Nazarene Youth Congress in Phoenix in the summer of 1995 and feeling the energy and commitment of 6,000 Nazarene teens, I am encouraged. After being with a number of our college presidents and district superintendents and sensing their vision and competence, I am encouraged. After being with hundreds of our younger missionaries and pastors and observing their spirit of sacrifice and evangelism, I am encouraged. With God's hand upon us, we are ready to boldly march into the 21st century with the message of full salvation through Jesus Christ.

—James H. Diehl
General Superintendent

It is very compelling to consider the strategic significance Christ has given His Church through His plan to evangelize the world. We in the Church of the Nazarene are a visible expression of the Body of Christ. As such, we have incredible responsibility for portraying Christ to the world. Additionally, we have the privilege of experiencing ultimate joy as His partners in miracles in this life and in being His "forever family" in the life to come. The Church has never in its history had greater opportunity for fulfilling Christ's plan for evangelism. Consequently, the Church of the Nazarene boldly steps through the millennial door of opportunity, expecting the greatest harvest of souls in the history of the church.

—Paul G. Cunningham
General Superintendent

There was a power and a passion present when the Holy Spirit came on the Day of Pentecost. That provided the impelling force to start the disciples in the arena that included the ends of the earth. It is evident, since the disciples and others could not accomplish the entire task, that Christ included succeeding generations, that in the mighty baptism of the Holy Spirit's power, they in their day should carry on until the end of time.

The Church of the Nazarene was born in that mighty power and thrust itself into the assignment given by Christ to His Church. Let us today carry on and on and on!

—V. H. Lewis
General Superintendent Emeritus

Without question the Church of the Nazarene was born in an outpouring of the Holy Spirit in genuine revival power! There is no other way to account for the phenomenal growth of a small company of 135 people into a church that now circles the world, numbering well over a million in membership.

As we enter a new millennium with hunger for His presence, let us humble ourselves and seek Him! He desires to come upon every heart, every Nazarene, and every church. Prevailing prayer is the route to real revival.

—Orville W. Jenkins
General Superintendent Emeritus

As a people of God, we must ever remember our reason for being. Founding General Superintendent Phineas F. Bresee believed that the Church of the Nazarene was raised of God to declare—to the Church Universal and the world—the "dispensational truth" that Jesus Christ baptizes us with the Holy Spirit to purify our hearts from sin and to perfect them in the love that He commanded in Matt. 5:43-48. Our God-given mandate, then, is "to spread scriptural holiness" to the ends of the earth.

—William M. Greathouse
General Superintendent Emeritus

The mission statement of the Church of the Nazarene and the Church Universal is one and the same—"Go and make disciples of all nations" (Matt. 28:19). I will always be grateful for the Nazarenes who led me to Christ and discipled me in the Santa Monica, California, church and at Pasadena (now Point Loma Nazarene) College. It has been a joyful privilege to perpetuate this mission by proclaiming full salvation for 52 years. The job description of every member of the Body of Christ, lay or ministerial, is still to make disciples through Holiness evangelism.

—Eugene L. Stowe
General Superintendent Emeritus

One hundred years ago Phineas F. Bresee, an effective Methodist minister, struggled to launch a new movement of biblical holiness that he labeled "the Nazarenes." Nazarenes of the 21st century are in a neodenominational era that requires ability to renew the characteristics of a religious movement. Institutionalism is not the answer, though a by-product. Market strategies of the world will not suffice, though innovation and the will to change are needed. Power and influence can come only with God's anointing to renew churches and to create thousands of new churches!

—Raymond W. Hurn
General Superintendent Emeritus

PHINEAS F. BRESEE
1838-1915
General Superintendent
1895-1915

I will sprinkle clean water on you, and you will be clean; I will cleanse you from all your impurities and from all your idols. I will give you a new heart and put a new spirit in you; I will remove from you your heart of stone and give you a heart of flesh (Ezek. 36:25-26).

Born in 1838 in Franklin Township, New York, Phineas F. Bresee was converted at age 18 and called to preach. He served as a Methodist minister from 1859 to 1894. After being associated with the Peniel Mission for a short time, Dr. Bresee, together with Dr. J. P. Widney, formed the first Church of the Nazarene in Los Angeles in October 1895 with 135 charter members. As other churches were formed and the organization became a national church in the unions of 1907 and 1908, Dr. Bresee served as general superintendent until his home-going in 1915.

God has called us to this work—to sacrifice and toil; to prayer and supplication; to proclamation and testimony. He has called us to a movement from which nothing can deviate us. We stand in the ranks; we wait around the throne. We march with fixed bayonets of flashing testimony. Nothing can turn us from the appointed way. We go onward to victory!

—Phineas F. Bresee
From his sermon "The Open Door" in "Sermons," 1903

HIRAM F. REYNOLDS
1854-1938
General Superintendent
1907-32

For this reason I kneel before the Father, from whom his whole family in heaven and on earth derives its name. I pray that out of his glorious riches he may strengthen you with power through his Spirit in your inner being, so that Christ may dwell in your hearts through faith (Eph. 3:14-17).

Hiram F. Reynolds, born in 1854 near Chicago, was converted at age 22 and called to preach the following year. He entered the ministry of the Methodist Church in the New England states. He attended Burr and Burton School, a Congregationalist college in Manchester, Vermont, for one semester and Montpelier Methodist Seminary in Montpelier, Vermont, for two years. In 1895 Dr. Reynolds united with the Association of Pentecostal Churches of America. He was elected home and foreign missionary secretary two years later. When the Association of Pentecostal Churches in the East and the Church of the Nazarene in the West united in Chicago in 1907, Dr. Reynolds was elected general superintendent to serve with Dr. Phineas F. Bresee. Reelected the following year at Pilot Point, he continued in this office until his official retirement in 1932. The General Assembly that year elected him to emeritus status, the first in the history of the denomination. For several years afterward, however, Dr. Reynolds continued presiding at district assemblies. During most of his active superintendency he also served as secretary for foreign missions and is largely responsible for the missionary passion and zeal so characteristic of the Church of the Nazarene.

I might say that this is not a perfection that makes one perfect in your physique; you have aches and pains in your body. Not a perfect knowledge, like Adam before the Fall. It is a heart cleansed from all inbeing of sin without which no man shall see the Lord.

—Hiram F. Reynolds
*From a sermon preached at
Providence, Rhode Island
March 29, 1931*

E. P. ELLYSON
1869-1954
General Superintendent
1908-11

"See, I will send my messenger, who will prepare the way before me. Then suddenly the Lord you are seeking will come to his temple; the messenger of the covenant, whom you desire, will come," says the LORD *Almighty. But who can endure the day of his coming? Who can stand when he appears? For he will be like a refiner's fire or a launderer's soap. He will sit as a refiner and purifier of silver; he will purify the Levites and refine them like gold and silver. Then the* LORD *will have men who will bring offerings in righteousness* (Mal. 3:1-3).

Edgar P. Ellyson is remembered largely for his work in education and Sunday School for the Church of the Nazarene. He was born of Quaker parents in Damascus, Ohio, on August 4, 1869, and was converted at age eight. In his early ministry he organized home mission churches, preached in camp meetings, and held revivals. Elected general superintendent at Pilot Point, Texas, in 1908, he served until 1911. He was president of or taught at Peniel, Pasadena, Olivet, Trevecca, and Bresee Colleges and was editor in chief of Sunday School publications from 1923 until his retirement in 1938. Dr. Ellyson authored six workers' textbooks on doctrine and methods for use in training Sunday School teachers.

Holiness is a state of rightness with God and with man, of purity of heart and of blameless behavior. It is not faultless, not freedom from temptation or mistake, not perfection of thought and action, but blameless as to motive, and pure in heart. It is not sinless as judged under the law, but is free from guilt as judged under grace; all guilt and pollution are gone.

—E. P. Ellyson
"Bible Holiness," 1938

E. F. WALKER
1852-1918
General Superintendent
1911-18

The LORD is compassionate and gracious, slow to anger, abounding in love. He will not always accuse, nor will he harbor his anger forever; he does not treat us as our sins deserve or repay us according to our iniquities. For as high as the heavens are above the earth, so great is his love for those who fear him; as far as the east is from the west, so far has he removed our transgressions from us (Ps. 103:8-12).

Edward F. Walker was born in Steubenville, Ohio, on January 20, 1852. He was converted at age 20 and soon thereafter was called to preach. He pastored both Methodist and Presbyterian churches. Before joining the Church of the Nazarene in 1908, he served as an evangelist. E. F. Walker pastored Pasadena, California, First Church of the Nazarene and was associate pastor under Phineas F. Bresee at Los Angeles First Church for a time. Later he served as president of Illinois Holiness University and then a subsequent term when it was known as Olivet College (today known as Olivet Nazarene University). He was elected general superintendent at the Third General Assembly in 1911 and continued in office until his death in 1918.

The Scriptures clearly and emphatically teach that sanctification is for converted people and for such only. Christ is represented as given for the world, that it might not perish; for the church, that He might sanctify it. Sinners are called to repentance; saints to sanctification. Pardon and life are promised the wicked who repent; transformation, life more abundant, are assured saints who consecrate. In the Word we find prayers for forgiveness of the guilty; for the sanctification of those at peace with God.

—E. F. Walker
"Sanctify Them," 1899

W. C. WILSON
1866-1915
General Superintendent
1915

His father Zechariah was filled with the Holy Spirit and prophesied: "Praise be to the Lord, the God of Israel, because he has come and has redeemed his people. He has raised up a horn of salvation for us in the house of his servant David (as he said through his holy prophets of long ago), salvation from our enemies and from the hand of all who hate us—to show mercy to our fathers and to remember his holy covenant, the oath he swore to our father Abraham: to rescue us from the hand of our enemies, and to enable us to serve him without fear in holiness and righteousness before him all our days" (Luke 1:67-75).

Born in 1866 in a farmhouse near Manitou, Kentucky, William C. Wilson was a Methodist pastor and evangelist before joining the Church of the Nazarene on the West Coast in 1903. He served the Church of the Nazarene as pastor and district superintendent until 1915. He helped establish three strong Nazarene churches in California at Long Beach First Church, Upland First Church, and Pasadena First Church. He also was involved in the creation of Nazarene University, now Point Loma Nazarene College. The Fourth General Assembly, meeting in Kansas City in 1915, elected W. C. Wilson as the fifth general superintendent of the Church of the Nazarene. His election marked the first time the denomination had four general superintendents at one time. Dr. Wilson died shortly after his election.

Let us linger at the mercy seat until we are anointed, baptized and fully prepared to go and publish the sweet and charming story of salvation; and under light and power of the Spirit, the truth we speak and live shall be caught up and wafted to every nation, touching every home, inspiring every tongue to sing the songs of His redeeming love.
—W. C. Wilson
"Our Equipments," 1896

J. W. GOODWIN
1869-1945
General Superintendent
1916-40

If you love me, you will obey what I command. And I will ask the Father, and he will give you another Counselor to be with you forever—the Spirit of truth. The world cannot accept him, because it neither sees him nor knows him. But you know him, for he lives with you and will be in you. I will not leave you as orphans; I will come to you (John 14:15-18).

John W. Goodwin was associated with Phineas F. Bresee in the founding of Nazarene University, which later became Pasadena College and is today known as Point Loma Nazarene College. Born in 1869 near North Berwick, Maine, he was raised in the Advent Christian Church. After moving to California in 1905, he joined the Church of the Nazarene. Dr. Goodwin served as pastor of the college church and as district superintendent of the Southern California District. When General Superintendents Bresee and Wilson died in late 1915, Dr. Goodwin and Dr. R. T. Williams were elected to the office. Dr. Goodwin served 24 years, until 1940.

The depth of spiritual life must be the measure of our spiritual vision and passion for others. We are not only to witness by telling the truth as what we know, but we are to witness unto Christ. This is something more than telling about Christ; the witness is unto Christ. Who is the Christ, but one who is holy, separated from sin and a Savior from sin? Then the true witness is one who is an example of Christ's saving power from sin. The power of the divine Spirit is the enablement to be a true witness. A Spirit-filled church is a witnessing church. A witnessing church is a missionary church. The baptism with the Holy Spirit gives the inward fire, passion to make known Christ's saving grace.

—J. W. Goodwin
"The Other Sheep," August 1938

R. T. WILLIAMS
1883-1946
General Superintendent
1916-46

Husbands, love your wives, just as Christ loved the church and gave himself up for her to make her holy, cleansing her by the washing with water through the word, and to present her to himself as a radiant church, without stain or wrinkle or any other blemish, but holy and blameless (Eph. 5:25-27).

Born in Milam, Texas, in 1883, Roy T. Williams was converted and sanctified at 16 and began preaching immediately. He was ordained by General Superintendent Hiram F. Reynolds at the Pilot Point, Texas, General Assembly of 1908. He was educated at Texas Holiness University, near Greenville, Texas (one of several parent institutions of Southern Nazarene University), where he was later professor of theology and Bible and president. He pastored Nashville First Church of the Nazarene for 3 years and then entered the evangelistic field. He and John W. Goodwin were elected general superintendents in early 1916, immediately after the deaths of General Superintendents Bresee and Wilson late the previous year. He served in this office for 30 years, from 1916 until his death in 1946.

The church needs powerful Christians; it needs hot Christians, those that pray with a fervent spirit. The church needs Christians full of peace and joy. But the outstanding need is purity—purity of mind, purity of word, purity of spirit, purity of character, purity of life. Give us multitudes of men and women who are so upright, clean, and pure in their hearts, their morals, and in their characters that no just charge can be laid against them by even their bitterest enemies.

—R. T. Williams
"Sanctification; The Experience and the Ethics," 1928

J. B. CHAPMAN
1884-1947
General Superintendent
1928-47

You were taught, with regard to your former way of life, to put off your old self, which is being corrupted by its deceitful desires; to be made new in the attitude of your minds; and to put on the new self, created to be like God in true righteousness and holiness (Eph. 4:22-24).

J. B. Chapman is one of the best-known names among the early general superintendents. He gave the church a rich legacy of Holiness literature and preaching. Born in Yale, Illinois, in 1884 and converted early in life, James B. Chapman began preaching at 16 and united with the Holiness Church, which in 1904 became part of the Holiness Church of Christ. He became a Nazarene through the union of the churches at Pilot Point, Texas, in 1908. He was a pastor and evangelist and served as president of two parent schools of Southern Nazarene University: Arkansas Holiness University in Vilonia, Arkansas; and Peniel University in Greenville, Texas (earlier known as Texas Holiness University). In 1922 he was elected editor of the *Herald of Holiness.* Dr. Chapman was elected general superintendent in 1928 and continued in this office until his death on July 30, 1947.

Sin and holiness are moral and spiritual antipodes, and one or the other must finally prevail. Sin and holiness cannot go on in mixed form forever. Either we must be saved from sin or sin will damn us forever. And this applies to all sin. There is no sin in heaven and no holiness in hell. This world is the place where we must make the abiding choice, and God proposes to allow our choice of sin to become fixed in impenitence or our choice of holiness to become effective by the power of His grace. This is the teaching of the whole tenor of the Scriptures.

—J. B. Chapman
"Holiness, the Heart of Christian Experience,"
1941

J. G. MORRISON
1871-1939
General Superintendent
1936-39

Create in me a pure heart, O God, and renew a steadfast spirit within me. Do not cast me from your presence or take your Holy Spirit from me. Restore to me the joy of your salvation and grant me a willing spirit, to sustain me. Then I will teach transgressors your ways, and sinners will turn back to you (Ps. 51:10-13).

Born in 1871 in Oskaloosa, Iowa, and raised in South Dakota, where he became a Methodist minister, Joseph G. Morrison was one of the founders of the Laymen's Holiness Association and served as its president until he joined the Church of the Nazarene in 1921. He was a district superintendent, president of Northwest Nazarene College from 1926 to 1927, and executive secretary of the Department of Foreign Missions from 1927 to 1936. Dr. Morrison was elected general superintendent in 1936 and served until his death in 1939.

A human soul thus entirely sanctified becomes the garden of the Almighty Gardener. With the pruning hook of His discipline, the plow of His chastisements, the showers of His grace, and the sunshine of His presence, there are brought forth the fragrant flowers of holiness that are a joy and delight to the owner of the garden.

—J. G. Morrison
"The Nazarene Pulpit," 1925

H. V. MILLER
1894-1948
General Superintendent
1940-48

I have given them your word and the world has hated them, for they are not of the world any more than I am of the world. My prayer is not that you take them out of the world but that you protect them from the evil one. They are not of the world, even as I am not of it. Sanctify them by the truth; your word is truth. As you sent me into the world, I have sent them into the world. For them I sanctify myself, that they too may be truly sanctified. My prayer is not for them alone. I pray also for those who will believe in me through their message, that all of them may be one, Father, just as you are in me and I am in you. May they also be in us so that the world may believe that you have sent me (John 17:14-21).

Howard V. Miller was ordained in the American Baptist Church and joined the Church of the Nazarene in 1922. Born in 1894 in Brooktondale, New York, he served as pastor, evangelist, district superintendent, and was dean of the School of Religion at Northwest Nazarene College at the time of his election to the general superintendency in 1940. Dr. Miller served the church in this capacity until his death in 1948.

Here is God's supreme challenge to His creature, His will for us, that we should come into such actual experiential relationship with himself that we can in reality worship Him in the beauty of holiness. Here is a beauty, not of inanimate quality, not a beauty granted His creatures arbitrarily, but a beauty that man, creature of will and intelligence, can possess and which will identify him with his God, bringing glory and praise to the One who made him.

—H. V. Miller
"His Will for Us," 1949

ORVAL J. NEASE
1891-1950
General Superintendent
1940-44; 1948-50

May God himself, the God of peace, sanctify you through and through. May your whole spirit, soul and body be kept blameless at the coming of our Lord Jesus Christ. The one who calls you is faithful and he will do it (1 Thess. 5:23-24).

Orval J. Nease served the church as evangelist, college president, executive secretary of the Department of Church Schools, and general superintendent. He was born in 1891 in Nashville, Michigan. He received his bachelor's degree from Pasadena College, his graduate degree from Boston University, and did additional graduate work at Ohio State University. Dr. Nease served the church as pastor of Phoenix First Church; Meridian, Texas; Malden, Massachusetts; Columbus, Ohio, First Church; and Detroit First Church. He served two terms as general superintendent: 1940 to 1944, and 1948 until his death in 1950.

Paul says . . . because you have divine love you ought to consecrate. He says you ought to consecrate by the mercies of God; and the mercies of God find themselves in the peace that you have with God, the access, the open heaven, and the present Christ; the fact that you rejoice in hope and have glory in tribulation, and the love of God shed abroad in your heart. He says you owe it to God, you owe it to life, you owe it to the church, you owe it to your home, you owe it to yourself, to give yourself in utter abandonment to God and His will!

> —Orval J. Nease
> *"The Meaning and Importance of Christian Consecration" in "A Vessel unto Honor," 1952*

HARDY C. POWERS
1900-1972
General Superintendent
1944-68

And a highway will be there; it will be called the Way of Holiness. The unclean will not journey on it; it will be for those who walk in that Way; wicked fools will not go about on it. . . . And the ransomed of the LORD will return. They will enter Zion with singing; everlasting joy will crown their heads. Gladness and joy will overtake them, and sorrow and sighing will flee away (Isa. 35:8, 10).

A native of Oglesby, Texas, where he was born in 1900, Hardy C. Powers was converted in the Alhambra, California, Church of the Nazarene and took theological training for the ministry at Pasadena College. After 12 years in the pastorate and 8 years as superintendent of the Iowa District, he was elected to the general superintendency in 1944 and served in this capacity until his retirement in 1968.

The message that brought the Church of the Nazarene into existence included all the generally accepted doctrines of Evangelical Christianity with a special emphasis on the doctrine of entire sanctification as a second work of grace, the heritage of all believers. The landmarks that have guided us in our journey for these 50 years may be like unto a mountain range. . . . Great pilot points to which they looked then and to which we look today. . . . First, the authority of Scripture. . . . To them the final arbiter of all manner of faith and practice was "What saith the Lord?" . . . Second, the adequacy of the Atonement. . . . Their ideal Christian experience was sins forgiven, the nature sanctified as a second work of grace subsequent to regeneration, and a holy, victorious life in this present world. . . . Third, the reality of Christian experience. . . . Theirs was a soul-satisfying, personal relationship to a divine personality. . . . It is time now to take our bearing once again by gazing at those mountain peaks of truth and principle that guided our founding fathers. They never change. They must never become unfamiliar to the people called Nazarenes.

—Hardy C. Powers
From his message at the Golden Anniversary celebration at Pilot Point, Texas, October 13, 1958

G. B. WILLIAMSON
1898-1981
General Superintendent
1946-68

Seek the LORD while he may be found; call on him while he is near. Let the wicked forsake his way and the evil man his thoughts. Let him turn to the LORD, and he will have mercy on him, and to our God, for he will freely pardon (Isa. 55:6-7).

Gideon B. Williamson was born in 1898 in New Florence, Missouri, was converted and called to preach at an early age, and joined the Church of the Nazarene in 1919. He graduated from John Fletcher College in University Park, Iowa, with further studies at McCormick and Northern Baptist Seminaries in Chicago. Dr. Williamson pastored for 16 years and served 9 years as president of Eastern Nazarene College. He was general president of the Nazarene Young People's Society from 1932 to 1940. In 1946 he was elected to the office of general superintendent and served until his retirement in 1968.

To possess spiritual soundness, or holiness, one must genuinely repent of his sins and believe on Christ as his Saviour. He must experience "the washing of regeneration, and renewing of the Holy Ghost." Furthermore, for the conscience to be fully awakened and sensitized, one must experience complete cleansing, which purges as by fire the moral judgment and causes one quickly, if not automatically, to "abhor that which is evil; cleave to that which is good."

—G. B. Williamson
"The Preacher's Magazine," August 1955

SAMUEL YOUNG
1901-90
General Superintendent
1948-72

But when the kindness and love of God our Savior appeared, he saved us, not because of righteous things we had done, but because of his mercy. He saved us through the washing of rebirth and renewal by the Holy Spirit, whom he poured out on us generously through Jesus Christ our Savior, so that, having been justified by his grace, we might become heirs having the hope of eternal life (Titus 3:4-7).

Samuel Young was a native of Glasgow, born there in 1901. He was converted under the ministry of Dr. George Sharpe and joined the Parkhead Church of the Nazarene in Glasgow. After coming to the United States with his parents, he graduated from Eastern Nazarene College and received a master of arts degree from Boston University. Dr. Young served the church as pastor, district superintendent, and president of Eastern Nazarene College. He was elected general superintendent in 1948, serving the church in this capacity until his retirement in 1972.

The people called Nazarenes believe that the cross of Christ is central in the redemption of mankind. They acknowledge the native sinfulness of man and the depravity of the whole human family. They do not aver that all men are as bad as they might be, but they do insist that no man in his own moral goodness is good enough. Everyone needs the saving grace of the Lord Jesus Christ through His atoning death on Calvary—the young and the old alike, the tender child and the case-hardened sinner. The Nazarenes believe that it takes the power of the Holy Spirit to convict men of sin. They also believe that this same Holy Spirit imparts to us in a personal way a sense of divine forgiveness and adoption when we have truly repented of our sins and believed in Jesus as Lord and personal Saviour.

—Samuel Young
"Herald of Holiness," March 11, 1953

D. I. VANDERPOOL
1891-1988
General Superintendent
1949-64

For this reason I remind you to fan into flame the gift of God, which is in you through the laying on of my hands. For God did not give us a spirit of timidity, but a spirit of power, of love and of self-discipline (2 Tim. 1:6-7).

Born in 1891 near Pollock, Missouri, Daniel I. Vanderpool was converted in a Free Methodist church in 1909 and began preaching in country schoolhouses within three months of his conversion. He joined the Church of the Nazarene in 1913. Dr. Vanderpool was educated at John Fletcher and Pasadena Colleges. Nineteen years in the pastorate and 14 years as district superintendent preceded his election to the general superintendency in 1949. He served as general superintendent until 1964.

Revivals have been and now are the genius of the Church of the Nazarene. Rugged preaching that calls for a clean break with the world and sin, and a strong faith in the Christ of Calvary; that calls for a full consecration of self, substance, and service to God; that gives promise of heart cleansing—all this accompanied by earnest prayers, watered by penitent tears, will precipitate outpoured revivals and will preserve the genius of the church and give an upward swing to the Crusade for Souls now.

—D. I. Vanderpool
"Herald of Holiness," March 11, 1953

HUGH C. BENNER
1899-1975
General Superintendent
1952-68

But the fruit of the Spirit is love, joy, peace, patience, kindness, goodness, faithfulness, gentleness and self-control. Against such things there is no law. Those who belong to Christ Jesus have crucified the sinful nature with its passions and desires. Since we live by the Spirit, let us keep in step with the Spirit (Gal. 5:22-25).

Hugh C. Benner had the distinction of being the first president of Nazarene Theological Seminary, elected to the position in 1944. He was born in 1899 near Marion, Ohio, and was converted at an early age. He graduated from Olivet College (now Olivet Nazarene University) and took further graduate work at Vanderbilt and Boston Universities and the University of Southern California. He served the church as a college professor at Trevecca, Eastern, and Pasadena Colleges, and later as a pastor at Santa Monica, California; Spokane, Washington; and Kansas City First Church. In 1952 he was elected general superintendent and served in this position until retirement in 1968.

Increase in scriptural knowledge, in spiritual discernment, in "effectual fervent prayer," in genuine manifestations of the presence of God, in the freedom of the Spirit, in experiential witness in the lives of our Nazarene laymen will produce strength, establishment, and achievement in Christian life and service and will help build that "glorious church" for which Christ gave himself.

—Hugh C. Benner
"The Nazarene Preacher," May 1965

V. H. LEWIS
1912-
General Superintendent
1960-85

On the last and greatest day of the Feast, Jesus stood and said in a loud voice, "If anyone is thirsty, let him come to me and drink. Whoever believes in me, as the Scripture has said, streams of living water will flow from within him." By this he meant the Spirit, whom those who believed in him were later to receive. Up to that time the Spirit had not been given, since Jesus had not yet been glorified (John 7:37-39).

V. H. Lewis was born in 1912 in Howell, Nebraska. After his conversion and call to preach, he graduated from Bethany-Peniel College (now Southern Nazarene University). He began his work in the ministry as an evangelist and traveled for eight years in the field of evangelism. After seven years in the pastorate and nine years as superintendent of the Houston District, Dr. Lewis was elected the first full-time executive secretary of the Department of Evangelism in 1956. He was elected general superintendent by the 1960 General Assembly and served in this office until his retirement in 1985.

Evangelism is . . .

. . . preaching the gospel of Jesus Christ to men everywhere.

. . . bringing people into a conscious knowledge of guilt before God.

. . . guiding souls into the act of repentance and the experience of the new birth.

. . . leading believers into a personal knowledge of the doctrine and experience of entire sanctification as a second definite work of grace.

. . . receiving Christians into the fold of the Church and building them up in the most holy faith.

. . . launching the spearhead of attack against the evil forces in the world.

. . . fulfilling the God-assigned task of the Church, the Great Commission in action.

—V. H. Lewis
"The Church Winning Souls," 1960

GEORGE COULTER
1911-95
General Superintendent
1964-80

Everyone who believes that Jesus is the Christ is born of God, and everyone who loves the father loves his child as well. This is how we know that we love the children of God: by loving God and carrying out his commands. This is love for God: to obey his commands. And his commands are not burdensome, for everyone born of God overcomes the world. This is the victory that has overcome the world, even our faith. Who is it that overcomes the world? Only he who believes that Jesus is the Son of God (1 John 5:1-5).

Samuel George Coulter was a native of Northern Ireland, born in 1911 at Magheraveely, County Fermanagh. At age 11 he moved to western Canada with his parents and two older brothers. He graduated from Northwest Nazarene College in 1933 and pastored churches in Canada, California, and Oregon. In 1948 he was appointed superintendent of the Northern California District, serving with distinction for 12 years. In 1952 Pasadena College conferred upon him the honorary degree of doctor of divinity, and for 7 years he served as chairman of its Board of Trustees. In 1960 he was elected executive secretary of the Department of Foreign Missions. Four years later, at the 16th General Assembly, held in Portland, Oregon, he was elected to the general superintendency. He retired in 1980.

The beauty of holiness in the sanctified becomes appealing to all observers and especially to spiritually oriented people who are seekers after Spirit-filled experience and life. In fact, the badge of authority to every Wesleyan-Arminian Holiness preacher is the beauty of holiness seen in the life that he lives. God declares through Isaiah, "How beautiful upon the mountains are the feet of him that bringeth good tidings, that publisheth peace; that bringeth good tidings of good, that publisheth salvation; that saith unto Zion, Thy God reigneth!" [52:7, KJV].

—George Coulter
"The Preacher's Magazine," April 1977

EDWARD G. LAWLOR
1907-87
General Superintendent
1968-76

Therefore, prepare your minds for action; be self-controlled; set your hope fully on the grace to be given you when Jesus Christ is revealed. As obedient children, do not conform to the evil desires you had when you lived in ignorance. But just as he who called you is holy, so be holy in all you do; for it is written: "Be holy, because I am holy" (1 Pet. 1:13-16).

A native of Yorkshire, England, Edward G. Lawlor was born in 1907 and later emigrated to Canada with his family. At the age of 30 he was converted from his family's Roman Catholic faith and subsequently joined the Church of the Nazarene. He conducted his ministry through the pastorate and the field of evangelism before being elected superintendent of the Canada West District in 1946. In 1960 he was elected executive secretary of the Department of Evangelism, where he served until 1968, when the General Assembly chose him for the Board of General Superintendents. He retired in 1976.

The message of the Prince of Peace has a timeless value; and this is our time to take this message the world around. Our task is to see that this message becomes the fulfillment of all the hopes and dreams of all mankind in this world of tension. Our task is to see that this message so excites us that we will go—to reap "the fields . . . white unto harvest." Our task is to see that this message so stirs us that in our own corner of this world of tension we add daily to the trophies of grace that we shall lay one day at the feet of the Prince of Peace, that day when every knee shall bow and every tongue confess that the Prince of Peace, Jesus Christ, is Lord to the glory of God, our Father. This is our task in a world of tension!

—Edward G. Lawlor
"Herald of Holiness," March 11, 1953

EUGENE L. STOWE
1922-
General Superintendent
1968-93

Therefore, I urge you, brothers, in view of God's mercy, to offer your bodies as living sacrifices, holy and pleasing to God—this is your spiritual act of worship. Do not conform any longer to the pattern of this world, but be transformed by the renewing of your mind. Then you will be able to test and approve what God's will is—his good, pleasing and perfect will (Rom. 12:1-2).

From 1944 to 1962, Eugene L. Stowe earned the reputation as a builder and masterful preacher while pastoring churches in Visalia and Oakland, California; Salem, Oregon; and College Church in Nampa, Idaho. This ministry undoubtedly prepared him for his denomination-wide responsibilities that were to come. He was born in Council Bluffs, Iowa, in 1922. In 1939 he transferred his membership in the Methodist Church to the Santa Monica Church of the Nazarene in California. He earned his baccalaureate degree at Pasadena College. Graduate studies followed at Pasadena and Berkeley Baptist Divinity School. From 1956 to 1960 Dr. Stowe was president of the Nazarene Young People's Society. In 1963 he accepted the superintendency of the Central California District, serving there until his election as president of Nazarene Theological Seminary in 1966. In 1968 the General Assembly elected him to the Board of General Superintendents, where he served until retiring in 1993.

Just as sin is twofold, so is salvation. John Wesley placed strong emphasis upon the fact that the Scriptures taught that full salvation consists of both justification and sanctification. The word "sanctification" means to be made holy. This process begins at justification. At the same time one is justified he is also regenerated or born of the Holy Spirit. This brings about a real as well as a relational change in one's life. The very fact that the Spirit of God is revealed as the Holy Spirit means that when He comes to dwell in the heart, He brings the holiness of God. Paul described it by saying, "If anyone is in Christ, he is a new creation; the old has gone, the new has come!" (2 Cor. 5:17).

—Eugene L. Stowe
From his sermon "David's Prayer for Full Salvation" in "Sanctify Them . . . That the World May Know," 1987

ORVILLE W. JENKINS
1913-
General Superintendent
1968-85

But if we walk in the light, as he is in the light, we have fellowship with one another, and the blood of Jesus, his Son, purifies us from all sin. If we claim to be without sin, we deceive ourselves and the truth is not in us. If we confess our sins, he is faithful and just and will forgive us our sins and purify us from all unrighteousness (1 John 1:7-9).

Orville W. Jenkins was born in Hico, Texas, in 1913. After studying prelaw at Texas Tech in Lubbock, he moved to central California, where he was converted in a small home mission church at the age of 22. Three years later, in 1938, he graduated from Pasadena College. At this time he began 24 years of pastoral work that included churches in Dinuba and Fresno, California; Topeka, Kansas; Salem, Oregon; and Kansas City First Church. While at Topeka, Dr. Jenkins was also enrolled in graduate studies at Nazarene Theological Seminary. In 1950 he was elected district superintendent of the West Texas District and served in this capacity for 9 years. He spent another 3 years as district superintendent of the Kansas City District and then became executive secretary for the Department of Home Missions in 1964. In 1968 the 17th General Assembly elected him to the Board of General Superintendents. He continued in this position until his retirement in 1985.

We believe that the Church of the Nazarene was brought into being by God as another outbreak of the fires of evangelism. In a day when the word "revival" was held in disrepute by many nominal Christians, the Church of the Nazarene was born in revival fires and proceeded to major in revivals. When other church groups had ceased using words such as "holiness," "heart purity," "entire sanctification," "perfect love," and "Christian perfection," the Church of the Nazarene conducted evangelistic services, preached on repentance and scriptural holiness. In the face of the liberalism, modernism, humanism, and materialism . . . the Church of the Nazarene has been urging forth the spirit of evangelism, which has marked God's peculiar people from Pentecost to the present day. With her emphasis on genuine conversion and heart holiness, the Church of the Nazarene has endeavored to maintain the evangelistic fervor and thrust of Pentecost.

—Orville W. Jenkins
"The Church Winning Sunday Nights," 1961

CHARLES H. STRICKLAND
1916-88
General Superintendent
1972-88

But we preach Christ crucified: a stumbling block to Jews and foolishness to Gentiles, but to those whom God has called, both Jews and Greeks, Christ the power of God and the wisdom of God. For the foolishness of God is wiser than man's wisdom, and the weakness of God is stronger than man's strength (1 Cor. 1:23-25).

Besides his 16-year tenure as general superintendent, Charles H. Strickland was well known in the church as the first president of Nazarene Bible College in Colorado Springs, elected to the position in 1967. Born in Cincinnati in 1916, he joined the Waycross, Georgia, Church of the Nazarene in 1928 at age 12. After attending Trevecca Nazarene College, he began his pastoral ministry in 1937. He served three churches in Georgia: Moultrie, Waycross, and Atlanta. After two years as Florida district superintendent and two years as pastor of Dallas First Church, he moved to South Africa in 1948. For 17 years he was district superintendent of the European work in that area. During that time he developed the Nazarene Bible College in South Africa, serving as its president for one year. In 1965 Dr. Strickland returned to the United States to oversee plans for the opening of Nazarene Bible College in Colorado Springs. In 1972 he was elected to the Board of General Superintendents. He remained a general superintendent until his home-going in 1988.

The mission of Christ was to provide a once-and-for-all atonement for sin—both in act and in nature—giving the people of the world a deliverance from sin. This deliverance involves both a forgiveness of actual sins and a cleansing of the sinful nature that is the root cause of action sins. Both are necessary to complete one's total redemption and to bring us into a complete acceptance with God.

—Charles H. Strickland
From his sermon "The Beauty of Holiness" in "Sanctify Them . . . That the World May Know," 1987

WILLIAM M. GREATHOUSE
1919-
General Superintendent
1976-89

Rejoice in the Lord always. I will say it again: Rejoice! Let your gentleness be evident to all. The Lord is near. Do not be anxious about anything, but in everything, by prayer and petition, with thanksgiving, present your requests to God. And the peace of God, which transcends all understanding, will guard your hearts and your minds in Christ Jesus (Phil. 4:4-7).

William M. Greathouse was converted during a six-week home mission campaign in Jackson, Tennessee. He joined the Church of the Nazarene in 1935 at age 16. Born in Van Buren, Arkansas, in 1919, he pursued several degrees during his early adult years from a number of institutions. From 1938 to 1958 he combined his scholarly responsibilities with those of pastor and teacher. During this 20-year span he completed degrees at Lambuth College, Trevecca Nazarene College, and Vanderbilt University; pastored Tennessee churches at Jackson, Franklin, Nashville (Immanuel), and Clarksville; and from 1955 to 1958 served as dean of religion and professor of Bible and theology at Trevecca Nazarene College while continuing his graduate study at Vanderbilt. In 1958 Dr. Greathouse accepted the pastorate of Nashville First Church, where he served until his election as president of Trevecca Nazarene College in 1963. In 1968 he accepted the presidency of the Nazarene Theological Seminary. Dr. Greathouse was elected to the Board of General Superintendents in 1976, where he served until his retirement in 1989. Since retirement Dr. Greathouse has been adjunct professor of religion at Nazarene Theological Seminary and distinguished professor of religion at Trevecca Nazarene University.

Jesus Christ, lifted up on the Cross, lifted up from the grave, lifted up to the throne of the Kingdom, is the world's only Saviour. He was lifted up to deliver us from the guilt and power of sin, to baptize us with the Holy Spirit, to come again in order to consummate our salvation and bring the final victory of God's rule in history!

—William M. Greathouse
"The Preacher's Magazine," February 1977

JERALD D. JOHNSON
1927-
General Superintendent
1980-97

For this very reason, make every effort to add to your faith goodness; and to goodness, knowledge; and to knowledge, self-control; and to self-control, perseverance; and to perseverance, godliness; and to godliness, brotherly kindness; and to brotherly kindness, love. For if you possess these qualities in increasing measure, they will keep you from being ineffective and unproductive in your knowledge of our Lord Jesus Christ. . . . Therefore, my brothers, be all the more eager to make your calling and election sure. For if you do these things, you will never fall (2 Pet. 1:5-8, 10).

Jerald D. Johnson was born in 1927 in Curtis, Nebraska, and was raised in a Nazarene parsonage. He graduated from Northwest Nazarene College in 1949 before serving as associate pastor at Spokane, Washington, First Church for two years. He then pastored churches in Coeur d'Alene, Idaho, and Eugene, Oregon. From 1958 to 1969 Dr. Johnson supervised the pioneering of the Nazarene work in Germany, Holland, and Denmark, in addition to helping organize European Nazarene Bible College. After moving back to the United States, he pastored the Cambrian Park Church in San Jose, California, and College Church in Nampa, Idaho, until his election in 1973 as executive secretary for the Department of World Mission. In 1980 the 20th General Assembly elected Dr. Johnson to the Board of General Superintendents.

His baptism is a cleansing, burning, sanctifying process that takes care of that which is called "carnal" and prepares a temple where He may indeed and in fact reside in all of His fullness. The coming of our Lord Jesus Christ, the sacrifice He made on the Cross has made it possible to receive the baptism of the Holy Ghost and fire. When fire is applied to the construction of wood, hay, stubble, gold, silver, and precious stones, the inevitable will happen. The wood, hay, and stubble will burn up, and what is left over will be gold, silver, and precious stones. When the fires of God in the baptism of the Holy Ghost and fire are applied to the carnal Christian, the inevitable will take place. Envy, strife, and divisions will be burnt up, and that which will remain will be a spiritual, a sanctified Christian, a true temple of the Holy Ghost.

—Jerald D. Johnson

From his sermon "Marks of Spirituality" in "Sanctify Them . . . That the World May Know," 1987

JOHN A. KNIGHT
1931-
General Superintendent
1985-

[A song. A psalm of David.] My heart is steadfast, O God; I will sing and make music with all my soul. . . . For great is your love, higher than the heavens; your faithfulness reaches to the skies. Be exalted, O God, above the heavens, and let your glory be over all the earth (Ps. 108:1, 4-5).

Born in Mineral Wells, Texas, in 1931, John A. Knight was converted as a boy and answered the call to preach as a student at Bethany-Peniel College (now Southern Nazarene University), where he graduated in 1952. After earning a graduate degree in philosophy from the University of Oklahoma, Dr. Knight became the first pastor of a home mission church in Columbia, Tennessee. Simultaneously he enrolled in Vanderbilt University, where he earned the bachelor of divinity degree and a Ph.D. in theology. His pastoral ministry was directed to four churches in Tennessee, the last one being Nashville Grace Church of the Nazarene in 1972. He was professor of Bible and theology at Trevecca Nazarene College, Mount Vernon Nazarene College, and Bethany Nazarene College. In 1972 he made the transition from the classroom to the presidency of Mount Vernon Nazarene College, and in 1976 he became president of Bethany Nazarene College. For a short interim between the two administrative positions, he served as editor of the *Herald of Holiness*. Dr. Knight was a member of the General Board from 1980 to 1985 and in June 1985 was elected the 25th general superintendent in Anaheim, California.

We believe God has raised up the Church of the Nazarene to bear witness to "entire sanctification." Our primary reason for existence is to assure men that "the blood of Jesus Christ . . . cleanseth . . . from all sin" (1 John 1:7 [KJV]). Our central and cardinal doctrine is redemption, or salvation, through Christ. This redemption is totally adequate to meet humankind's deepest spiritual need. The atonement of Christ when appropriated by repentance and faith, and/or consecration and faith, not only nullifies the works and manifestations of sin—that is, sins and sinning—but the condition of sin itself, the in-being or inner sin. The salvation of Christ deals both with the symptoms of sin and with the disease itself.

—John A. Knight
*From his message "The Holiness Pulpit"
in "Go . . . Preach," 1992*

RAYMOND W. HURN
1921-
General Superintendent
1985-93

Love must be sincere. Hate what is evil; cling to what is good. Be devoted to one another in brotherly love. Honor one another above yourselves. Never be lacking in zeal, but keep your spiritual fervor, serving the Lord. Be joyful in hope, patient in affliction, faithful in prayer (Rom. 12:9-12).

Raymond W. Hurn was born in Ontario, Oregon, in 1921. During his developmental years, he experienced the pioneering of two new churches by his parents, Walter and Bertha Hurn. A graduate of Bethany-Peniel College (now Southern Nazarene University), he also pursued graduate studies at Tulsa University, Oklahoma University, and Fuller Theological Seminary. He was ordained in 1943 by General Superintendent H. V. Miller. For 16 years he served pastorates in the following churches: Hays, Kansas; Tulsa, Oklahoma, Central; Atlanta, Georgia, First; Norman, Oklahoma, First; and Medford, Oregon, First. He was superintendent of the West Texas District for 9 years. In 1968 he was elected executive secretary of the Department of Home Missions. Throughout the 17 years in home missions he was very active in developing ethnic work and in stimulating local churches to start new works among ethnic groups. He spearheaded a new thrust in church planting in the denomination. He has authored several books and under his leadership a bimonthly tabloid, *Mission Alert,* was published as a church growth resource. Dr. Hurn was elected the 26th general superintendent in June 1985 at the General Assembly in Anaheim, California. He served in this position until his retirement in 1993.

"Holiness" is the one single word that best describes the meaning of the apostle's phrase "walking in the light." It is living a life that is in sympathy with holiness. But more than that, it is a walk that creates within us a heart that beats in total harmony with the light of God. The life becomes the practice of holiness. Inward principles and beliefs are expressed in outward behavior. The one who is walking in the light is progressing in holiness, not stationary but advancing.

—Raymond W. Hurn
*From his sermon "Joy in the Family"
in "Sanctify Them . . . That the World May Know,"
1987*

WILLIAM J. PRINCE
1930-
General Superintendent
1989-

May the God who gives endurance and encouragement give you a spirit of unity among yourselves as you follow Christ Jesus, so that with one heart and mouth you may glorify the God and Father of our Lord Jesus Christ. . . . May the God of hope fill you with all joy and peace as you trust in him, so that you may overflow with hope by the power of the Holy Spirit (Rom. 15:5-6, 13).

William J. Prince's involvement in the church has included a wide variety of assignments, from pastoral ministry in California, Minnesota, and Ohio to the superintendency of the Pittsburgh District. He is a native of Altus, Oklahoma, where he was born in 1930, and is a graduate of Bethany-Peniel College (now Southern Nazarene University) and Nazarene Theological Seminary. Dr. Prince extended his services to the international scene through teaching and preaching missions in Haiti, Central America, Africa, and other world areas. From 1970 to 1976 he was rector of European Nazarene Bible College in Schaffhausen, Switzerland. In 1980 he became president of Mount Vernon Nazarene College, and in May 1989 he was elected to the presidency of his alma mater, Southern Nazarene University in Bethany, Oklahoma. The 22nd General Assembly, however, wielded a prior claim by electing him the 27th general superintendent for the church in June 1989.

There is no doubt that God has called the Church of the Nazarene to be His instrument of salvation. We cannot fulfill His calling to us without prayer and personal witnessing. We cannot accomplish it by human strength or human skills. We can accomplish His will only as we remain willing workmen set afire by the Holy Spirit. Our good works and plans and great programs cannot substitute for the outpouring of His Holy Spirit in our midst. Tears for the lost, intercession for the wayward, prayer for repentance, and willingness to surrender "all" to Him—that brings revival and conviction. Let us pray for ourselves, for one another, for a personal and worldwide outpouring of the Holy Spirit to empower preaching, to reach families and communities around the world for our Lord Jesus Christ.

—William J. Prince
From his message "Evangelism and Preaching" in "Go . . . Preach," 1992

DONALD D. OWENS
1926-
General Superintendent
1989-97

I want to know Christ and the power of his resurrection and the fellowship of sharing in his sufferings, becoming like him in his death, and so, somehow, to attain to the resurrection from the dead (Phil. 3:10-11).

Donald D. Owens has been a pastor, missionary, educator, and author. He was born in Marionville, Missouri, in 1926. For 13 years, beginning in 1954, he was a missionary in Korea, where he helped establish Korea Nazarene Theological College. He earned a Ph.D. in anthropology after returning to the United States and taught anthropology and missions at Bethany Nazarene College and Nazarene Theological Seminary. Later he accepted a new missionary assignment in the Philippines, where he was the founding president of Asia-Pacific Nazarene Theological Seminary and the first regional director of the Asia-Pacific Region of the Church of the Nazarene. He has written four books on the church's mission outreach and responsibilities. In 1985 Dr. Owens was elected president of MidAmerica Nazarene College in Olathe, Kansas. He served there until 1989, when he was elected the 28th general superintendent.

Preaching is an event in which the living Word of God is proclaimed in the power of the Holy Spirit. Preaching, real preaching, is a dynamic, divine-human interaction traceable to God's prompting and power, and that takes place for God's own reasons and not from our desire to be in "top form." Jesus promised His disciples that the power they saw at work in Him was available to them as the Holy Spirit came upon them. We who are called to serve ought to have an abiding infilling of the Holy Spirit. When we are anointed with the Holy Spirit, all of our being is made available to God for service. Such anointing enabled Jesus to speak, not just as the scribes, but as the fountain of truth.

—Donald D. Owens
From his message "The Preacher as a Person" in "Go . . . Preach," 1992

JAMES H. DIEHL
1937-
General Superintendent
1993-

May the God of peace, who through the blood of the eternal covenant brought back from the dead our Lord Jesus, that great Shepherd of the sheep, equip you with everything good for doing his will, and may he work in us what is pleasing to him, through Jesus Christ, to whom be glory for ever and ever. Amen (Heb. 13:20-21).

James H. Diehl was born in Des Moines in 1937 and was raised in an Iowa Nazarene home. He received his bachelor's degree from Olivet Nazarene College in 1959. He was ordained on the Iowa District in 1960. Dr. Diehl pastored for 21 years, serving congregations at Muscatine, Iowa; Indianola, Iowa; Oskaloosa, Iowa; Atlanta First Church; and Denver First Church. He served for 10 years as district superintendent of the Nebraska and Colorado Districts. From 1973 to 1976 he served as assistant to the president at MidAmerica Nazarene College. In July 1993 the 23rd General Assembly elected Dr. Diehl the 29th member of the Board of General Superintendents.

Keep the flame burning! Don't settle for cold ashes when you could have blessed fire. If Timothy needed to fan into flame the gift of God, how much more urgently do we need the same in this modern day of blatant secularism, materialism, and sin. May God fan into flame the fire of the Holy Spirit in Nazarene churches across America and across the world! My soul cries out for holy fire in our hearts and churches.

—James H. Diehl
"Herald of Holiness," June 1994

PAUL G. CUNNINGHAM
1937-
General Superintendent
1993-

Praise be to the God and Father of our Lord Jesus Christ, who has blessed us in the heavenly realms with every spiritual blessing in Christ. For he chose us in him before the creation of the world to be holy and blameless in his sight (Eph. 1:3-4).

Paul G. Cunningham came to the general superintendency from nearly 30 years as senior pastor of College Church of the Nazarene in Olathe, Kansas. Born near Chicago in 1937, he is a graduate of Olivet Nazarene College and Nazarene Theological Seminary. He was ordained on the Kansas City District in 1965. A longtime member of the General Board, Dr. Cunningham was its president from 1985 until his election as general superintendent. He has held various positions in the church, including chairman of the Board of Trustees of Nazarene Theological Seminary and secretary of the Board of Trustees of MidAmerica Nazarene College. The 23rd General Assembly in Indianapolis elected Dr. Cunningham the 30th member of the Board of General Superintendents in July 1993.

Jesus had a profound sense of time. He knew His time was short, so He remained focused on His mission. Jesus said in Acts 1:8 "You will receive power when the Holy Spirit comes on you." In other words, our power source comes first, and then we will have the energy necessary to be effective disciples. First and foremost, regardless of time demands, we must be in connection with our power source in order to have energy for evangelism. Jesus told His disciples the number one priority was to wait for the promise of the Father to be fulfilled in their own lives. With His empowerment, they would then be enabled to carry out His mission to win the world. Our world has never been in greater need of a Savior. The fatal disease we war against is sin. Its cure is found through emancipation of the soul. This will be accomplished by energized disciples who have disciplined themselves to wait before the Father until His promise of empowerment becomes a personal reality. Could we ask for a double portion of the Holy Spirit's power that we might have lives of significant influence? Life is so short. Everything is at stake. Let's keep the main thing the main thing and so order our lives that we can receive adequate power to be energized disciples.

—Paul G. Cunningham
"Herald of Holiness," July 1996